TRIBE OF THE NORTH CENTRAL NIGERIA

Idris Ele-ojo

THE IGALA'S

An African history

TRIBE OF THE NORTH CENTRAL NIGERIA

THE IGALA'S

AN AFRICAN HISTORY

BY

IDRIS ELE-OJO

CONTENTS:

Introduction

The Igáláà are one of Nigeria's ethnic groups. Kogi state's Idah serves as the capital. Kogi state is home to the majority of Igala people. They may be found in the Kogi state local governments of Idah, Igalamela/Odolu, Ajaka, Ofu, Olamaboro, Dekina, Bassa, Ankpa, omala, Lokoja, Ibaji, and Ajaokuta.

Benue State, Anambra State, Benue and Enugu States, as well as the Niger River, which separates the kingdom from Edo State, comprise the kingdom's northern, southern, eastern, and western borders, respectively. It should be remembered that the Bassa Local Government Area, which includes Bassa Nge, Bassa Komo, and Mozum, was governed as a division of the Igala Kingdom from 1918 until 1977. It is located within the same angle as the Niger and Benue rivers.

The historical growth of the kingdom is critically dependent on the strategic environment. The Igala have extensive interaction with the Ibo, Yoruba, Edo-speaking peoples, and Jukun, to mention just a few major groups, due to their geographic location. It is evident from the documented accounts of the nineteenth-century explorers that Idah, the capital of the Igala, is located on the Niger River.

Igala people have historically been farmers who grow a wide range of local crops, including yams, taro, pumpkins, squash, corn (maize), manioc, and peanuts (groundnuts). For the Igala people, palm oil and kernels are both major cash crops. The Igala people worship "Ojo," the all-powerful divinity. They see the Ojo as the Igala people's traditional conception of God. because he is revered as the All-Powerful, who gave the gods and spirits authority over many facets of human existence. These gods and spirits engage with mankind directly on a daily basis. The Igalas continue to follow Ifa, their ancient religion, nevertheless.

CHAPTER 1

ORIGIN

The Igala inhabit an area of open savannah vegetation to the north and a belt of deciduous woodland to the south. The region is located in Nigeria's warm, humid climate zone. There is a clear dichotomy during the wet season. The dry season runs about from October to the end of March or early April, whereas the rainy season typically lasts from approximately April to the end of September or early October. Heavy rains and the harmattan's consequences might occur, particularly starting around November. With the big rivers (Benue and Niger), a few smaller ones like Okula, Ofu, Imabolo, Ubele, Adale, and Ogbagana, as well as other streams across the area, the vegetation is mostly deciduous. As a result, Igalaland is renowned as a fortunate fishing and agricultural location.

They reside in a triangle-shaped area of land near the meeting point of the Niger and Benue rivers. Like many other ethnic groups in Nigeria, the Igala have a number of myths and traditions around their alleged site of birth. As many traditions as there are researchers who have tried to uncover the origin of the people have resulted from various efforts to trace their history.

Idah in the current Kogi state serves as the ancestral home and administrative center for the Igala people. Additionally, Attah Igala's seat is in Idah. The highest monarch of the Igala people worldwide is Attah Igala, also referred to as the Attah of all Igala people. Attah Igala, HRM (Dr) Agabaidu, the current

Idakwo Ameh Oboni II is the 82nd Attah Igala to have reigned since the end of the ninth century AD. Despite archeological evidence that the Igala moved to Idah approximately 500 BC, inadequate recordkeeping made it impossible to get the list of Attah Igala prior to late 0900 AD.

The language is a member of the Niger-Congo family's Benue-Congo branch. The Bassa Nge and the Bass Nkome, who reside between the Igala and the Benue River, were two more tribes that their traditional ruler, the ata, oversaw. Politically, traditional Igala civilization was structured as a kingdom. Kings conducted lavish courts attended by a large number of officials and attendants, many of whom were slaves and eunuchs; they were divine and surrounded by several taboos. Every heavenly kingdom in Africa had traditions that served as limits on the king's authority. This featured a tradition in which the queen mother—the only person permitted to do so under the taboo system—could reprimand the king.

Agana- Poje, the father of Idoko, replaced Ebule- Jonu, a woman, as the first "Ata," the title given to the head of the country. Atiyele, the first son of Idoko, moved eastward of the kingdom to build Ankpa kingdom, while Ayegba, the second son of Idoko, replaced his father as Ata'Gala. Idoko would subsequently succeed him as Ata and have two children, Atiyele and Ayegba om'Idoko (Ayegba son of Idoko). He oversaw a conflict with the Jukun that was successful. In December 2012, Idakwo Micheal was chosen to serve as the next Ata. Four lineages of the royal dynasty alternated holding the ata-ship of Igala. In the seventh century, Abutu-Eje established the Igala Kingdom. The holy Earth shrine is guarded by nine elite officials known as the Igala Mela(9), who served as the kingdom's rulers.

Northern Igbo states were colonized by Igala between 1450 and 18th century.

Midway through the 17th century, the Igala megastate was at the pinnacle of its reputation. The transatlantic slave traffic was diverted from the Bight of Benin to the Bight of Biafra as a result of the establishment of the Igala mega state, which also had a role in the fall of the Benin Empire during the sixteenth and seventeenth century. The Idah-Benin War (1515–16) was an independent conflict between the two nations. Later, when it became a major exporter of choral beads, horses, medicine, talents, and, of course, slaves to the coastal area, the Igala state attained its political and economic dominance. However, the dynamics of the previously complicated connections with a number of northern Igbo villages were altered by its expanding influence. In 1797, Joseph Hawkins had previously documented Igala raids on some far northern Igboland.

He recorded the escalating hostilities between the "Ebo Country" and the "Galla" in "A History of a Voyage to the Coast of Africa." The Igalas had influenced several of the indigenous northern Igbo mini-states' socioeconomic, political, and religious spheres by the late 17th century. The Igala held sway at Asaba, Opi (an archeological site), Nsukka, Nsugbe, and a number of Igbo settlements on the Anambra River and lower Niger. Onitsha's trading outpost and the Ijo middlemen were well-established. Several Igala warriors contributed to the development of the Igala colonial takeover of these northern Igbo nations, including the legendary Omeppa, Inenyi Ogugu, who established a stronghold at Opi (an ancient site). But Onoja Oboni, the renowned Igala warrior and slave trader, was the one who had the most effect on the development of Igala-Igbo influence in the 18th century.

Over time, legendary iconography has obscured Onoja Oboni's individuality and background. Including being the Son of Eri, the Grandson of Aganapoje, or a member of the priestly sub-clan of Obajeadaka in Okete-ochai-attah, one of the Idah royal lineages. He was a skilled strategist, a slave robber and trader, a conqueror, a colonizer, and an imperialist, which are the main points of agreement. His diplomacy, expansionist tendencies, and cultural acculturation of conquered lands were added to them.

Recent archaeological discoveries of the residue of his fort's ruins on the premises of the University of Nigeria Nsukka prove that he constructed himself a walled city in Ogurugu. The forts and defenses that the Igala troops constructed extended from Ete all the way down to Opi (an ancient site), and then on to Anambra. The history of the Igbo communities on the Anambra River and the Lower Niger during the Igala economic and socio-cultural ascent and control was impacted by Oboni's rise to power, as was the history of the North-Western Nsukka. The Igala empire's golden era of imperial growth was being reinforced during the time. In this fashion, the Igala mega state seized power and received pledges of fealty. The Ezes of Enugu-Ezike, Akpugo, Nkpologu, Ibagwa Ani, and Opi continued to obtain their titles from Idah up to the collapse of Igala authority; investiture, installation, and confirmation of their position could only be accomplished with Attah Igala's royal blessing in Idah.

The Eze were only considered legitimate when they came home with Igala choral beads, or "aka," which were said to have magical charms to preserve their longevity and safety as well as a prestige animal (a horse) to boost their pride. Periodic royal trips to the Attah Igala were also made in order to pay respects, improve diplomatic relationships and contacts between groups, reaffirm loyalty, and provide protection from slave raids. The Igala soldiers introduced arrowheads with sting ray poison at the tip, ironworking, carving, cloth knitting, terracing of the Nsukka hillsides, and well-developed political and social hierarchies in addition to building factories (forges) for manufacturing Dane-guns and other indigenous technologies.

Igala Empire had developed into a center for cultural interchange at this period; it had an impact on civilizations as far away as the Nok Civilization in the north and the Igbo-Ukwu Civilization in the east. Many parts of the Igala-Nsukka borderland continue to speak two languages. In terms of religion, the Igala appointed their own priests—the Attama—as the keeper of the hazardous Alusi shrine, assumed control as the communities' liaisons with the supernatural, oversaw divinations, and created "Ikenga" and "Okwute" (ritual staffs) that combined Igala and Igbo religious elements. As a result, the Attama were the primary Igala sociocultural control agents.

Even while the formal Igala identity is still prevalent, several attempts to retain the Attama lineage Igala failed, leading to a significant igbonization of the priestly position. Many of the northern Igbo state villages have ancestors with Igala names, as well as cultural customs that have been significantly modified and adapted. Even now, people still prefer using Igala circular baskets than Igbo rectangular ones. The Igala empire was too big at the turn of the 19th century for any dependable, strong central rule. Internal degradation and collapse started.

The Igala have traditionally been an agricultural people that cultivate a broad variety of regional crops, including as yams, taro, pumpkins, squash, corn (maize), manioc, and peanuts

(groundnuts). Both palm oil and kernels are becoming important cash crops.

Since 1865, Christian missionaries have operated among the Igala, converting a number of people in the cities and bigger villages; Islam, however, continues to be the dominant religion.

CHAPTER 2

ORIGINS OF IGALA ACCORDING TO SOME PREVIOUS RESEARCHERS AND HISTORIANS AND WHY THEY ARE ALL FALSE OR NOT CORRECT

i. Jukun origin:

Igala people or the reigning family are said to be of Jukun origin, according to Miles Clifford (1936). Due to Igala migration from Wukari to Idah, Jukun in modern-day Wukari, Taraba, was thought to be of Igala origin. Palmer (1936) claims that when the warriors Ahel Dirk moved to the region, a group of people known as the Ahel Gara (natives), today known as Gala/Igala/Ngara, resided in the Benue Valley (Taraba state). An Ahel Dirk of Kanem branch founded themselves on the Benue at Wukari and named the

They discovered natives there named Gara (which, by a typical metathesis, became Gala). This demonstrates that Igala people were already there before other people joined them, thus it will be wrong to claim that the one (Igala) who was already before the other (Jukun) arrived would have its origins in the latter comer (Jukun).

Igalamela and Igala-ogba people had already been living in Idah for a very long time before Abutu Ejeh, together with Idoko, Agana Apoje, Amichi, Idoma group, founders of Kakanda, Ebira people,... came to Idah. As a result, numerous Attah Igala governed Igala people before Abutu Ejeh arrived from Wukar Because his forefathers stayed in Wukari while other Igalas moved to Idah, Abutu Eje was mistakenly labeled as having Jukun ancestry. As a result, he grew up there among other Igala until he had to go to Idah after a considerable amount of time. The names Amichi (the quiet or humble one), Ejeh (the leopard denoting bravery), Idoko (a male child born when the father is not at home; on the farm, or went fishing or hunting), and Abutu (a male child born after several searches including the mother taking various herbs), are all Igala names to date and are not found among the Jukun. With the exception of the remaining Igala, they really have no idea what these terms imply, much alone use them as names.

Additionally, outside of Kogi state, almost all indigenous Igala communities in Nigeria have Igala traditional titles, such as Attah of Obosi in Anambra state, Attah of Odekpe in Anambra state, Attah Okakwu of Igbedor in Anambra state, Okakwu of Ossamala in Anambra state, Akor of Aika in Delta state, Akor of Oko in Delta state, Onu

Additionally, Attah Igala has stated that Igala originated in Egypt near the Nile river on numerous occasions; one of these times was during the Igala National Congress that he hosted on February 15, 2020 in his palace in Idah, Kogi state, where he informed the gathering of indigenous Igala delegations from six states that Igala migrated from Egypt near the River Nile to Wukari and then to Idah.

Aku Uka of Wukari, the Jukun people's traditional leader, was recently interviewed by the Ashe Foundation, a social and cultural organization in Nigeria. Therefore, it may be said that Jukun's origins as a member of the ruling class or an Igala are wholly untrue.

ii. Yoruba origin:

After visiting Idah, the Igala people's ancestral home, in 1854, Bishop Samuel Ajayi Crowther wrote in his book (A comparative word-list of Yoruba, Igala, and English) that "Igala was a Yoruba sovereign who had lost his territory to Fulani invaders and ran to Sultan of Nupe for assistance to enable him to have a new habitat. The Sultan then purchased the property and appointed a Yoruba man as Attah. Was he implying that the Fulani or Sultan had installed the Yoruba as a people to dominate a region at that time? Was or is Attah a Fulani, Hausa, or Yoruba traditional title? Wherever a Sultan installed a monarch, was the title distinct from that of an Emir? In addition, it was Igala, not Lokoja, Ajokuta, Itobe, or Okpachala, let alone someone who would have traveled to Idah, who conquered Queen Amina of Zazau in Zaria and had her murdered and buried. Is there any traditional leader in southwest Nigeria who has the title Attah currently or in the past, apart from Attah of Ayede in Ekiti who is linked to Igala and has Attah as his title?

Before the collective name Yoruba was given to them as their tribe, were the Southwestern region of Nigeria not made up of Igala, Omooduduwa/Ife, Nupe/Igala (who even ruled Oyo for almost a century when they chased Oyo ruling dynasty away), Olukumi/Igala, Egun, Ijesha, Itsekiri, Returnees from outside Nigeria after abolition of slave trade Can any of the aforementioned statements be supported by evidence? No! But Samuel Ajayi was the "Eyes" of the white people back then, therefore whatever he saw and told them was accurate.

In actuality, here is an online dictionary: www.meriam-webster.com>. "The Yoruba-speaking people on the Niger at its confluence with Benue in Nigeria" is how the dictionary defines Igala. This was all down to Bishop Ajayi Crowther's fraudulent record, which led certain indigenous Igala people outside of Nigeria, such the Nago people of Brazil, to believe they were Yoruba even though the name "Nago" is of Igala origin and does not even have a meaning in Yoruba. The claim that the Igala people originated from Yoruba should also be rejected since all of the aforementioned were untrue and can never be shown to be accurate.

iii. Benin origin:

Boston (1962) and Sergeant (1984), citing the Benin account of the Igala origin, claimed that the Igala reigning dynasty had its roots in Benin. The Igala/Idah Benin battle was said to have been waged by Attah Aji, one of the preceding Attah Igala, who was also a Benin hunter and the brother of the then-Oba of Benin, Oba Esigie. They characterized the conflict as a struggle between two brothers, Esigie, the Oba of Benin, and Aji, the Attah Igala. Is Aji even a Benin name, though? Even now, many Igalas still go by the name Aji, but no one goes by that name in Benin, and if they do (which hasn't been discovered yet), they don't even know what it means. In Igala, the word aji is used to refer to "the young, persons of recent character or conduct, vigor, or power." That being said, it is documented, especially by the Portuguese, that the Benin-Idah (Igala) bordered the territories of Attah Ayegba Oma Idoko's Igala and Oba Esigie's Benin.

In addition to being documented, the Igala-Benin War occurred in 1515–1516 and was the conflict in which Attah Ayegba Oma Idoko buried his daughter, Princess Inikpi, alive. Princess Inikpi's statue has been standing at her gravesite in Idah, Kogi state, along the Niger River, since the time of her burial. So when did Aji engage in combat with Oba Esigie? Was Ayegba a Benin or maybe Oba Esigie's brother? The solution is no!

Another story added that Igala was from Benin and that Attah Igala was the monarch of that country because of the Ejubejuailo (pectoral mask) medal that he wore. This was also incorrect since the medal, which Attah Igala continues to wear today, served as a reminder of the Igala warriors' first-ever victory against the Benin people.

There were two Igala (Idah)-Benin wars. The first was brought to the palace of the Oba of Benin by Igala troops as revenge for forcing back

Igala settlers who, according to the Oba, were growing or advancing towards Benin across the Niger River on the opposite side of Idah. The Igala warriors stormed the Oba's palace, vanquished the palace guards, and removed the Oba's pectoral mask from him to Idah, which is still Attah Igala's Ejubejuailo today.

The second war was the Benin's act of retaliation, and since they knew the Igala were unbeatable, they had to use Portuguese mercenaries and high-powered weapons that the Igala warriors' local weapons could not withstand. As a result, the Igala adopted a spiritual strategy as instructed by the gods, which resulted in the sacrifice of Princess Inikpi, which caused spiritual fire to "burn down" the Benin. Later, it was determined that Idah was not really burning, but rather that Idah was coated with the princess's blood, which seemed to be fire.

Therefore, the claim that the Igala originated in Benin is false; neither Ayegba nor Aji were inhabitants of that country. In conclusion, the medal was not handed to the Igala but rather accepted by Igala warriors as a symbol of triumph. Additionally, the Benin-Igala conflict took place under Ayegba as Attah Igala and Esgie as Oba of Benin, not Aji, making it wholly fictitious and deserving of being disregarded.

Ejubejuailo (pectoral mask)

REAL ORIGIN OF IGALA

The Igala tribe originate from ancient Egyptians. Several accounts from Egyptologists and ancient Egyptian archeologists, including some of the following, have supported this.

First, "The third Dynasty, The Dynastic Egyptians, according to Sir Harry Johnson, "were not far removed from the Galla [Igala] of today," Lewis Spence, around 1915

2. "... the third Dynasty that preceded the fourth has a highly Ethiopian aspect in Sa Nekht; the 12th Dynasty (1991–1802 BC) we may link to a Galla [Igala] Origin,..." 1927's Petrie Flinders

3. Oxford W.E, 1915, "According to Professor Sergi of Rome,... the ancient Egyptians belonged to Nubians, Abyssinians, Galla [Igala], Masail, Somali,..."

4. According to UNESCO, the prehistoric inhabitants of the Nubian Nile valley from the predynastic era to the first dynasty belonged to a race that included Bejas, Galla, Somalians, Nubians, and others.

5. "The Galla, a group now residing in southeast Africa, down the Nile and settled at Qua, where they formed the tenth Dynasty of Egypt," 1931's Petrie Flinders

The 18th and last Pharaoh of the 10th dynasty was Merikara of Igala (Gala). The meaning of Merikara is "The Beloved of the Spirit of Ra." The name Ra, which means "might and strength," was given to the sun deity.

Between 2075 to 2040 BC, he was in power. In other words, Igala existed from the dawn of time until the predynsatic era, which began about 6000 BC and ended approximately 3150 BC, when Egypt was formed.

The fact that countless Igala terms and words from ancient Egypt still have the same meanings centuries after our exodus is another evidence of the Igala language's Egyptian roots. The wearing of earrings by Attah Igala and Ancient Egyptian Pharaohs, as well as the wearing of white and red crowns by Attah Igala and Ancient Egyptian Pharaohs, the same crowning procedures for Attah Igala and Ancient Egyptian Pharaohs, the same procedures for burying any transited Attah Igala and Ancient Egyptian Pharaohs, including his excursion by servants (though no longer done in Igal

They (Igala) left Egypt when Egypt began experiencing problems like famine, after participating in the formation of Egypt (unification of lower Egypt (Igala location near River Nile) and upper Egypt) in 3150 BC, and participating in the rulership/Pharaoh council in the third dynasty (2686 BC - 2613 BC) i.e. 73 years, ruling as the tenth dynasty from 2130 BC to 2040 BC for 90 years, and

After Egypt was conquered by the Kush Kingdom in the eighth century BC (0700 BC), several communities, notably the Igala, left Egypt. Since they were fishing and residing along the Nile, as we are now along both banks of the river Niger, Igala traveled by a variety of ways and in some instances with the assistance of their boats. They eventually arrived in what is now Wukari, in Taraba state, and made themselves comfortable before additional groups began to join them. Two Igala groups migrated from Wukari to Idah (Opuata and Igalogba) around the 6th century BC (0500BC), according to archeological evidences, after remaining in Wukari for nearly two centuries (200 years) and the population of Igala increasing significantly. These two Igala groups are the modern-day Igalamela (Etemahi, Onubiogbo, Egwuola, Onede,...)

After a considerable amount of time, the first two Igala groups in Idah were joined by certain Igala clans that had remained in Wukari as well as several Igala sibling tribes including Idoma, Alago, and Ebira, commanded by Abutu Ejeh. However, as previously indicated, Igala had existed and was one of the few tribes whose names appear on the old list of tribes of ancient Egypt, as shown by the aforementioned archaeological evidence. As a result, Igala is one of the very few old tribes in Nigeria and all of Africa. Because we were likely the first or one of the first few tribes in Nigeria, native Igala territory may now be found throughout 29 states of Nigeria and the FCT.

Gala became Igala due to our practice of prefixing every word that doesn't begin with a vowel with "I." Many Igala people still pronounce Peter, Motor, Cup, Paul, and Buhari as Ipeter, Imotor, Ipaul, Ibuhari, and Igala, respectively.

The Attah Igala, AgabaiduIdakwo Ameh Oboni II, has said several times that the Igala people came from Egypt somewhere near the Nile. In one conversation, he said that he had learned through certain Jukun elders and other trustworthy papers that Igalas had already been in Wukari before the Jukun people had arrived. His Majesty, Attah Igala also stated that Igala migrated from Egypt through various places, including Borno state to Wukari where Igala settled with some tribes before they migrated to Ife and then to Idah to form a new territory. This was during the historic Igala reunification festival, Igala National Congress, which was hosted by the Attah Igala in his palace in Idah, Kogi state.

CHAPTER 3

Tradition and politics

The Attah-Igala, a supreme king who is revered as the ancestor of all Igala people, serves as the top of the political structure, which is focused on the monarchy. The ancient Attahs were incredibly powerful and formed a very strong empire that may have been around in the 8th or 9th century AD. At its height, possibly in the 16th century, the Igala kingdom did reach far and wide, encompassing portions of Igboland (Nsukka Area) in the south, Koton-karfe (including and beyond area of north Kogi) in the north, western Idoma land (including Igumake) in the east, and portions of Etsakor in the west.

At Nri-Igbo-Ukwu and Onitsha in Anambra state, among the Nembe and Kalabari on the Atlantic coast, as well as Asaba and among the Nupe in modern-day Niger state, where an Igala prince, tosede or Edgi is credited with founding the Nupe kingdom, the Igala, operating from their headquarters at Idah, were also felt. With these and other people, wars were fought, peace treaties were signed, tributes were paid, and commerce was formed. Wars, for instance, were fought with the Jukun of Kwararafa in modern-day southern Taraba State and with the Benin in 1515 and 1516 AD, according to Portuguese documents found in Lisbon at the time.

The British effectively colonized the region that is now known as Nigeria starting around 1890. The British policy of what is now known as Nigeria, where established monarchs were used to rule their own people "indirectly," was disrupted with the union of the Northern and Southern Nigeria protectorates in 1914 (by Col. Frederick Lugard). As a result, the authority of the kings and chiefs steadily diminished until they were reduced to puppets in the British hands. Although there were pockets of resistance, such as in Opobo (led by Jaja), Itsekiri territory (led by Nana), Benin (led by Overanwen), Sokoto (led by Sultan Attahiru), and Igalaland (led by Prince Atabo Ijomi, afterwards known as Ata-Igala from 1919 to 1926), the traditional rulers ultimately lost the war.

The kings were made tutelary heads of the administrations and native administrators were set up (roughly along geo-ethnic lines), with the British serving as the true administrators and decision-makers. In keeping with this, even after gaining independence in 1960, the Kabba province continued to govern the Igala native authority.

When a twelve state system was established, Igalaland became the eastern portion of a Kwara State (formerly titled Central Western State) with the arrival of the military in 1966 and the foundation of the state in 1967. Igalaland was separated from Kwara and joined as the Western portion of a new Benue State when a new nineteen-state structure was subsequently constructed out of the twelve in February 1976. The nomadic Igala arrived in Kogi, a new state, in August 1991, which is where they now remain.

Idah continued to serve as the Igalaland's cultural center and the Idah Local Government Area's seat of government. Igalaland was divided into three administrative divisions in 1968 for practical reasons. Idah, Ankpa, and Dekina units were governed by local governments until later (in 1976). Again, local government units were cut from Ankpa, while Ofu was cut from Idah. The Dekina division was separated into Dekina and Bassa. Nine of the 21 local governments in Kogi State are now located in Igalaland.

THE IGALA TRADITIONAL COUNCIL

There used to be one Igala traditional council headed by the Attah. Later, with the creation of an autonomous local government area, and Ankpa traditional council headed by Eje was created. A Bassa Komo, Bassa Nge and the Ebira Mozum Districts with its headquarters at Oguma was also recognized. Dekina and Idah remained under the umbrella of the Igala traditional council headed by the Attah-Igala. In the present dispensation, each local government council in Kogi state has its own council of Chiefs and everyone recognizes the pre-eminence of their respective premier monarchs — the Attah-Igala, the Ohinoyi-Ebira and the Obaro of Kabba.

THE IGALA MONARCH

The Attah-Igala, who is revered and recognized as the father of the Igala people, has a major position in the Igala Monarchy, one of the most powerful and ancient in central Nigeria. Although the exact historical location of the Attah institution has not been established, oral tradition and archaeological evidence suggest periods between the eighth and ninth centuries AD.

The Nri and Igbo Ukwu cultures, the latter of which has been dated to the 8th and 9th centuries AD by Professor C. Thurstan Shaw, may have been affected by the Igala royalty. If so, it might be inferred that the beginnings and history of the Igala culture predate the 8th or 9th century AD (Shaw, C.T. 1970, Igbo Ukwu, Faber, London).

Oral history claims that certain Attahs who cannot be identified chronologically ruled over "Igalaland" for a long length of time. Agenepoje, Abutu-Eje, and Ebole Jonu are a few of them. However, this is a highly tumultuous time in the history of the Igala monarchy, whose duration and distance have not yet been determined.

The Chief Imam of the palace, Alh. Idrisu Liman, leads the Special Jumm'at Prayer before HRM, AMEH OBONI II begins work for the day's chores. Ayegba Oma Idoko, the founder of the current quadrilinear dynasty, lived at an era following the proto-dynastic one when oral tradition was much more trustworthy. As a result, the Ayegba's descendants, led by Akwumabi, Akogwu, and Ocholi, have produced the Attah Igala in succession throughout time. The lineage of the Akwumabi dynasty was later divided into two groups, Ame-Acho and Itodo Aduga in charge of each, resulting in a four-dynasty structure.

In order to decentralize power, the kingdom was divided into smaller pieces with the help of Atta Ayegba Om'Idoko in the seventeenth century A.D. The British then established the districts in 1905. Ankpa, Dekina, Egwume, Ejema, and Imane were among these districts. Ogwugwu, Iga, Ika, and Ojokwu. Ife, Biraidu (Abocho), Atabaka (Okpo), and (Abejukolo). Okenyi, Ojokiti, Odu, Iyale, Emekwutu, The "traditional titles of "Onu" were given to these regions when they were established and "trustworthy relatives and followers" were appointed to lead (the principal person or chief).

According to an Igala legend, an Atta gave the Nupes a kingdom and gave Edegi (Tsoede), one of his sons from a Nupe mother, the right to control the Nupe nation. His gifts were a bronze canoe, twelve Nupe slaves, and the bronze Okakachi (Trumpet), which is still in use by Northern Nigerians. He also gave him numerous kingly symbols. Tsoede or Edegi subsequently assumed leadership of the Nupe people and adopted the title of Etsu (King), and the Nupe kingdom joined forces with Igala. The Staate drums were draped with brass belts and hefty iron chains and fetters that were blessed with great mystical power.

TRADITIONAL PATTERNS

The Igala are patrilineal, and the males hold the positions of power in the family or clan. Patilineality among the populace mysteriously necessitates virolocal living, in which the wife relocates to her husband's home among his paternal or, sometimes, his maternal kinsmen. The original Igala civilization was essentially polygamous, therefore the nuclear family—which consists of a husband, his wife, and their offspring as well as any associated kin—was seldom seen in those communities.

In order to produce more children whose assistance was desperately required on the farm, males who were farmers had to marry additional women. A man's riches and rank were also sometimes reflected in polygamy. The compound family, which consisted of a man, his women, and kids, was more common. The larger and more enduring patilineal joint family, which often consists of two or more generations of brothers and sons, as well as their spouses and children, is what the nuclear and compound families are in reality. Igala families are long-lasting and self-sustaining in this manner since the loss of one member has no effect on the group's structure as a whole. It may have a membership of up to 100 people or more, and it can continue for numerous generations.

An Igala lineage consists of multiple extended families, including the spouses and children of brothers, the wives and children of these brothers' fathers, and all other relatives of one's father's brothers.

In addition to having a shared name and identity, exogamous marriages, land ownership, mutual economic and political support, and protection from a competitor or aggressor among other things, the clan is made up of various patrilineally connected extended families or lineages. They acknowledge different ceremonial restrictions, such as taboos on specific foods, totems, etc., that give them a feeling of oneness and set them apart from other people since they are related and have a claim to a shared lineage.

KINSHIP RELATIONSHIP

Among the Igala, the idea of kinship thrives. It has aided in the creation of long-lasting social organizations where the concept of shared "blood" creates strong bonds between members who are closely related. Additionally, these groupings may assert exclusive rights to clan and lineage property by asserting exclusive ancestry. Each member of this form of kin connection benefits from a feeling of stability and self-identity. In the traditional Igala culture, familial relationships are significant because they affect people's access to land for farming, their ability to marry or engage in sexual interactions, and their standing in the community. Additionally, it encompasses much more than just kinship or domestic relationships. Individual families are required to fulfill certain tasks and obligations within a network of duties and support.

Generic phrases like "uncle," "aunt," or "grandfather" are sometimes insufficient for describing familial relationships among the Igala; instead, more precise expressions like "my maternal uncle" or "my maternal aunt" are used to distinguish between patrilineal and matrilineal relatives. Lineal relationships—those between grandparents and their grandchildren—are highly valued. The same rules apply to relationships with uncles, aunts, cousins, nephews, and nieces as with those biological relatives. The maternal kin relationships are strong among the Igala. Although a "daughter" is cared for, protected, and given many advantages, the paternal clan is the only one with the right to inherit. Lines of descent, residency, property inheritance, marriage, and other factors are all tied to kinship connections and obligations to lineal, collateral, and affinal kins (i.e., parent-in-law, children-in-law, and sibling-in-law, as well as with partrilineal and martrilineal kin).

INCEST TABOO

Any cultural or social standard that forbids practices of sexual relations between relatives is known as the "incest taboo." Where there are no tracable genealogical links, relationships among clan members are acceptable. However, where there are blood ties, sexual relationships between members of different clans are prohibited. The prohibitions on inter-family marriage and sexual relations in Igalaland are founded on a general sense of decency and a firm conviction in the integrity of blood ties. There are guidelines for acceptable and unsuitable sexual relations, however they are not written down. Incest, which is sexual activity between people who are distantly related, is forbidden. It is thought that if a man engages in an improper sexual connection with a relative, both parties would have terrible ailments from which they won't be able to recover until they own their wrongdoing and the gods are suitably appeased by sacrifice. It could also lead to a bleak landscape. Both would suffer a loss of public respect as people would stop taking them seriously. Young females that engage in such behavior now seldom married in the past.

Because the Igala are patrilineal and believe that children belong in the father's clan, persons who are connected to one another in various ways—and sometimes distantly—are categorized as siblings, while others who are genetically just as closely linked are not considered kin. Relationships between father and daughter, mother and son, uncle and niece, etc. are deemed incestuous as a result of patrilineality, while in certain matrilineal societies this may not be an issue. A man's relationship with his mother's sister and her daughter is seen as incestuous. Similar to this, a man and his father's sister are not permitted to engage in sexual activity, get married, or even have children together.

CHAPTER 4

TRADE AND COMMERCE IN IGALA LAND FROM THE PRE COLONIAL PERIOD

Trading networks on a local and regional scale played a significant role in the economy. It should be noted that the two systems weren't mutually exclusive. Actually, there was a continuity between them, particularly when talking about an economy as tiny as that of its neighbors, like Aboh and Edo. It is important to keep in mind that, while trade and commerce during this time weren't always as organized and sophisticated as they are now, they still showed an effort on the part of the populace to transform natural resources and use them to create economic networks that would keep them in constant contact with their immediate surroundings. Later, as a result, Ane Igala was plotted along the Niger on the map of the economic powerhouse.

A diversity of game flourished due to the Ane Igala's (with particular reference to the Ibaji) position between the high rain forest and the Savannah woods. These comprised, among many other animals, elephants, buffaloes, bush cows, leopards, antelopes, and wild pigs. Professional hunters developed their talents via rituals, strategies, hunting in various places under various circumstances, and specializing in a certain kind of animal. These games were traded in the marketplaces, which helped the populace's economy. Because some of the forest products were included into the regalia of the governing dynasties, it also elevated the Igala. For instance, the tusk of the elephant, which is used to make ivory, was of great value. Additionally, certain animals' bile and venom were used as medicines.

The many weapons employed in these games of hunting were essentially just pieces of rudimentary gear that represented how humans interacted with nature and the advancements in mechanical and chemical methods. As a consequence, humans devised the bow, deadly arrows, and toxic swords in an effort to subdue nature. These were produced nearby and given as trade goods to neighboring farmers and hunters. Guns made locally were also produced and distributed by them. The arrival of weapons, ammo, and European firearms led to an increase in the sophistication and ferocity of hunting practices. As a result, there are now more games available at the bank market, in both quantity and variety.

Commercial activities, namely those related to trade and marketing, have long been a part of Igala culture. The many types of agricultural products in the various Igala land zones acted as a significant trade stimulant. The hierarchical state system, the river Niger and its ties to other populations in the Nigerian area as well as to foreigners like the Arabs and Europeans, all facilitated trade. The Igala were one of the most significant trade groupings in and around the area even before the 19th century. The strategic position of the Igala territory allowed them to trade directly and indirectly with the Ebirra, Afenmai, Esan, Nupe, Igbo,

Benin, Yoruba, and many other tribes thanks to vast networks along the River Niger, i.e. the Egga port and the nearby hinterland. In fact, this region had significant agricultural surpluses and was well known for its premium fish, rice, yams, colors, and palm oil. They took advantage of the intricate political, economic, and religious relationships that existed between the Esan/Benin, Aboh, and Onitsha Igbo and Nupe populations.

Producers traded goods for those they did not make themselves internally. Slaves, salt, fish and other marine resources, as well as carved artefacts for religious use, dominated the regional commerce and are heavily represented in Igala re-exports. Slaves were traded heavily in pre-colonial commerce in addition to food items and other household items. The Igala warriors, according to Northrup, had provided the region with slaves. Some were bought at local marketplaces like Panda, Ikiri, Gbobe, Asaba, and Aboh, while others were acquired via raids and tribute. Additionally, slaves arrived from Kakanda and Nupe. It was said at the beginning of the 19th century that Ikiri market sold roughly 11,400 slaves yearly, the most of them were from Nupe and Kakanda.

Men and women both took part in trading in pre-colonial Igala. The capture and sale of slaves, as well as the trade and sale of horses, dogs, and other animals, were of greater significance to men. Additionally, they engaged in regional commerce, security services, large-scale trade organization and finance, and product exports. They also engaged in wholesale and brokerage activities. Because there were so many trees in the Igala woods, the males were particularly skilled carvers. Thus, in addition to carving mortar and pestles for pounding oje (cassava flour), they also made sacred artifacts (ebo) for both internal use and trade. According to Biakie's study, the Igala were well-served by the carving business, which he said was quite profitable. A boat that was twenty feet long and eight feet wide was selling for fifty cowries in 1850, according to Baikie, which was enough money to hire a beautiful female slave. Due to the limits imposed by the guild, the market for canoes was fairly constrained and included elements of governmental monopoly, ensuring substantial profits. Because fisherman and merchants transported their agricultural products up to Edo, Aboh, and other nearby trading regions, Highland boats were in high demand. Due to the increasing demand, specialist canoe builders began to appear, which helped the industry advance to some extent.

By the middle of the 19th century, the Igala had also given other fishing villages (on the Edo side of the river and beyond) various fishing instruments including net and fishing hooks in addition to the boats they had made for transporting their wares to and from the market and for interconnection. To increase profit, this was created by the populace and governed by the authorities. Additionally, management of the net was necessary to avoid a scenario in which juvenile fish would be trapped, causing a boom in one year.

Periodic marketplaces were held by the Igala societies. A week typically consists of four days since the Igala traditional week was computed based on market days. Each local market had commercial activity on each of those days. The commercial operations were conducted so as not to conflict with those in other locations. The Niger Bank Market in Illushi, with its commercial activity at the Egga-Oria or the Niger Bank, was the most significant of them, however.

Because of its proximity to the Niger River, merchants from nearby communities brought their products to the market and bought Igala wares. Some European goods that found their way into the interior of the settlements around the river Niger came from this market as well. The cowrie money, which was brought to the Ane Igala via the river Niger bank market, is a good example of this.

The bank market at Illushi serves as a meeting place for merchants from Aboh, Igbo land, Esan, Onitsha and Itsekiri, Usobo and Benin, as well as Nupe traders from the North. It is located at the boundary between Edo and Igala country. Periodic marketplaces provided for the entry of merchants from a distance, fostered the collection of a range of trade goods, cut down on the amount of time needed for marketing, and enabled customers to visit almost every market in a given region in turn. The expenses of collecting and distribution were decreased by the markets' regular meetings.

CHAPTER 5

PRE-COLONIAL POLITICAL ADMINISTRATION IN THE IGALA KINGDOM

Since the majority of recent scholarship has concentrated on the political systems of the three largest ethnic groups—the Hausa/Fulani, Yoruba, and Igbo—there seems to be an intellectual conspiracy against the lesser ethnic groups. This dissertation attempts a discourse on the pre-colonial political administration of North Central Nigeria; a study of the Igala political kingdom in an effort to preserve these tiny ethnic groups from political extinction. Secondary data were used to create the data for this investigation. The paper is divided into several but related sections. The article discovered that under Ayegba Om'Idoko, the process of the development of dynasty authority that had begun in the 16th century had become more cemented, and as a result, this served as our beginning point. After conquering the Jukuns, Binis, and Hausa/Fulani jihadists, the article concludes that the Igala political monarchy was the only most powerful kingdom during the 16th and 18th centuries. Given this, the Igala political kingdom cannot be ignored but rather must be recognized and recorded for political history and future generations.

Out of the more than 300 ethnic groups that make up the nation, there is a tendency for biased recording of the pre-colonial political administration in Nigeria, even among indigenous researchers (Hausa/Fulani, Igbo, and Yoruba political pre-colonial system). As

Abdullahi (2006) noted, of the three major ethnic groups identified in Nigeria by the slogan WAZOBIA, the WA in it means come in both Yoruba and Igala, but little is known about the pre-colonial political administration of the Igala kingdom. This suggests that there is an intellectual conspiracy against the minority ethnic groups, including the Igala kingdom. This work uses the Igala Kingdom as its starting point to investigate the pre-colonial political administration of one of Nigeria's so-called minor ethnic groups, situated in the North Central geopolitical zone. The Igala Kingdom's argument is based on the observation that, despite the fact that pre-colonial administration existed in Nigeria prior to the arrival of colonialism, efforts have focused on the larger ethnic groupings as though the lesser communities had a recognized system of government.

For instance, had noted that even before the start of colonization, the inhabitants of what would eventually be known as Nigeria were living under various forms of political and administrative structure. On the other hand, it was said that it would "need a deep understanding of the following important pre-colonial institutions in Nigeria." The Yoruba, Hausa/Fulani, and Igbo pre-colonial political systems are noteworthy. Therefore, as Coleman(1986) remarked, there is a propensity for the smaller, more dispersed tribes to lose their identity and incline toward the dominant groups, notably the Hausa. In actuality, however, Coleman (1986) had highlighted that the forest belt was home to around seven distinct black kingdoms before colonization, including the Ashanti, Dahomey, Ife, Oyo, Bini, and Jukun (Apa) Kingdoms. Consequently, this essay makes an effort to explain the Igala kingdom's pre-colonial political structure.

The Igala Kingdom is the ninth-largest ethnic group in Nigeria out of the country's roughly 300 ethnic groups, and it has played a significant role in the nation's history. It is one of the few ethnic groupings that has close ties to Nigeria's three main ethnic groups. In addition, Ocheja (2011) claims that out of the more than 300 major languages that are currently spoken in Nigeria, Igala orthography (alphabetical writings and accurate word spellings) is one of only about twenty-seven that has been approved by the National Educational Research and Development Council (NERDC) of the Federal Ministry of Education.

The Pre-colonial Political Administration of the Igala Kingdom. In the pre-colonial era, the Igala had a system that was rather strong, and throughout the colonial and post-colonial eras, they even joined forces with other ethnic groups to establish the Kabba province. The province was a part of the Northern region until 1967, at which point it split into Kwara and Benue, until becoming a part of Kogi in 1991. Ijoma (2007) noted that, of all the accounts, it is the role of Ayegba as the creator of the system of hereditary title on which Igala political organization depends. Although the available literature has shown that there were three (3) proto dynastic periods before the emergence of Attah, Ayegba Om' Idoko, the central theme is that, of all the accounts, it is the role of Ayegba as the creator of the heredit In addition, Ukwedeh (2003) noted that under Ayegba Om'Idoko, the process of the dynasty rule's development, which had begun in the 16th century, had solidified about the middle of the 17th century. Under this dynastic system, there existed a system of succession within the same royal family rather than the transfer of power between the many Igala-Mela patrilineages.

In what is now known as Nigeria, the Igala kingdom was a pre-colonial West African nation. The Igala, an ethnic group dwelling to the north of the Igbo with its capital at Idah, established the kingdom. Ayegba Om' Idoko is the name of the autonomous Igala kingdom's first Attah (Father) (Ayegba the son of Idoko). The Attah, who represents a father figure, is the ruler of the Igala. The entire title of the king, Attah Igala, which means the father of Igalas, comes from the term attah, which means father. The monarch, known as Attah, who held the office of a unique sovereign and served as the source of all patronage and justice in the realm, was and remains at the top of traditional, social, and political structure.

Particularly during the Igala-Jukun War, the governance of the Igala kingdom under Attah Ayegba represented a great reform of the country. He overhauled the advisory council, the Palace, and the district administration in addition to the central administration. Ayegba Om' Idoko left behind a strong central government, a peaceful society, and a flourishing economy (Onucheyo,2005:13). In the old Igala pre-colonial political system, the king had two distinct roles: first, he served as the head of the royal clan, and second, he oversaw a centralized system of territory administration. On the one hand, he was the ultimate custodian of the natural land shrine known as Erane, which represented the moral and spiritual welfare of Igala as a member of the same political community, and on the other, he was connected to the royal ancestors whose cult was one of the central themes of the Igala traditional religion. The Attah Igala, a single institution, combines many political and ceremonial roles, nevertheless. As Boston(1968) correctly noted, territorial considerations are of utmost importance in the administrative system by which the Igala are currently governed, and the division of the kingdom into districts and village areas would form a natural starting point for any analysis of the modern system of government. It is interesting to observe that in the Igala kingdom, agnatic linkages are used to decide who would hold hereditary political positions as well as the other statuses involved in the inheritance of rights over people and property. The Olopu patrilinear groupings, whose members held power over succession and inheritance, are the hereditary bodies of the Igala kingdom. According to Boston (1968), these are the organizations who dominated public and political life in the old system and are still the focal points of most of Igala life today. The district political administration of the Attah Ayegba was organized using the following models.

ATTAH

■

DISTRICT OFFICERS (ONU)

■

CLAN HEADS (GAGO)

■

VILLAGE HEADS (OMADACHI)

■

YOUTH LEADER (OCHIOKOLOBIA)

It might be claimed that the Igala mela communities' decision to unite as a corporate body marked the beginning of the Igala administration. Like the current governor, who is known as Onu, each village had a leader who served as the general head of the group. The local chiefs were given freedom to manage the affairs of their territories, but instances and concerns about the succession to local thrones were sent to the kingdom's capital, Idah, for Attah's consideration. Ascension occurs via heredity and genetic factors. A district would be made up of many villages, each of which would have a village chief in command of several villages. District levels of governance follow a similar structure to Idah, the capital of the kingdom. A portion of the tribute they collected was delivered to Idah, while the remainder was utilized to maintain the province. They were in charge of all district matters to the greatest extent feasible, although instances of murder, deposition, and succession were sent to the Attah at Idah. Attah Ayegba chose his sons, dependable relatives, and supporters to lead the district administration. As it was not feasible to rule the whole kingdom directly from Idah at this time, the district chiefs likewise decentralized and assigned tasks and power.

The Igala political system is structured on clans, and as such, the head of a clan (Onu) performs the same administrative duties as a royal province chief, including keeping the peace and collecting tributes in the areas under their control. the management of the palace. There were two kinds of officials in the Attah's palace: the Attah's eunuchs (Amonoji), who were in charge of running the palace, and the royal servants known as (Amedibo). These palace leaders carried out the following duties: they guarded the Attah, encouraged the populace to repair homes and the palace walls, sent communications to the regions, and collected tributes for the Attah. They served as a go-between between the Attah and both his chiefs and his subjects. They also guarded the treasures, regalia, and robes of the Attah. The eunuchs conducted ceremonies for the Attah and guarded the Attah's women. The Attah's court was presided over by Ogbe, the head of the Attah judicial court, who also briefed the Attah on the proceedings.

Attah's palace administration was based on democratic principles. For instance, in Igala, it is often said that: Onu noja oja n'onu (meaning the

King owns the people and the people own the king). The Attah operated a decentralized system of government with council members like today's minister in different areas and portfolio respectively. The Atah's Councilors. Within the reigning lineage, the body of royal councilors represented both the Atta's own direct line of descent and the various collateral branches. In relation to the ruling house itself, the council formed a council of elders often referred to as Abogujo Olopu. The council as Boston (1968) has noted was the executive body and corporate representative of the ruling house and in a wider sense, the functions of the councilors are sufficiently well defined. The councilors also acted as intermediaries, Ohiegba, between the locality concerned and the central government in judicial, political and other matters. The titled (portfolio) councilors were also responsible for mobilizing the royal army in time of war and on major expeditions accompanied the king into the field as the head of their own contingent.

JUDICIAL FUNCTIONS

The provision of justice to its residents has always been one of the most important duties of governments across the globe, from the ancient to the modern eras, and the Igala political kingdom was not exempt from this duty as it provided judicial services to its people. Throughout Idah, the Igala kingdom's capital, as well as in the provinces, disagreements between individuals and groups were arbitrated in front of family leaders. Heads of both groups and families worked to find common ground in order to resolve disputes amongst families in order to maintain peace and stability.

The village leaders, known as Omadachi and Gago, handled divorce cases, property disputes, and other minor matters, while instances of murder and treason were strictly left in Attah's hands. In the districts, the district rulers known as the Onu wielded both judicial and administrative responsibilities. The highest court, Attah's court (Ogbede), was situated in front of Ede market and held public hearings every day. In spite of the fact that Ogbe, a senior eunuch, took over as president of the court since Attah was unavailable due to a number of obligations, Attah was the official president of the court. Ogbe served as the court's president and rendered verdicts in straightforward, minor issues; the Attah was tasked with handling major situations. According to the documents that are now available, Ochalla Angna and Olimamu Attah, two Islamic clerics who functioned as court scribes (what are now known as court clerks), preserved and recorded court proceedings in Arabic. As few incidents are anticipated to be reported to the police, this technique was and continues to be exceedingly successful. Acrimony and animosity that may develop from incidents reported to the police were kept to a bare minimum.

DEFENCE OF THE KINGDOM

Unlike the modern state where we have standing army, the Igala kingdom had no standing army but there was initiation preparedness where adults were initiated and weapons were amassed awaiting any eventuality. Weapons such as arrows, bows, cutlasses, spears, shields and charms were abundantly stored in the armory. In the absence of standing army, servants, attendants, slaves and a large numbers of local farmers were mobilized and deployed for operation during wars. In the Igala political kingdom, Attah's chief were at the head of those local armies but in serious wars such as the one between the Igalas and Jukuns, Attah himself would lead the battle.

The Decline and Collapse of the Igala kingdom.

The decline and collapse of the Igala kingdom began in the 18th Century and finally collapsed and lost its sovereignty and independence in 1900. Both internal and external factors gave rise to the collapse of the Igala kingdom as there was no established written constitution with binding sanctions on the people across the entire kingdom. Internally, the sheer size of the kingdom contributed immensely to its collapse. As the kingdom began to grow in size, it became more difficult to keep the distant districts under the full control of the Attah due to poor communication and logistics of that period. Another internal factor that led to the collapse of the Igala kingdom was the absence of a constitution binding on all the districts that constituted the kingdom. The Igala kingdom was a loose state where the district heads in the north east for instance exercised a kind of autonomy thereby making the Attah to lose grip over the entire kingdom. The third factor that contributed to the collapse of the Igala kingdom was the breakup of Igalamela. With the breakup of Igalamela, Igalamela chiefs were removed from state advisory council on the ground that the Attah Ameh Ocheja accused the Igala mela chief of assassinating his predecessor Attah Ekelega and replaced them with royal councilors. Consequently, the Igalamela chief who had checked the excesses and activities of the oppressive Attah could not perform this function after their removal from the council

The last internal factor was the collapse of the Igala state economy. The decline of the slave economy which was the main stay of the Igala state economy contributed immensely to the collapse of the kingdom. The Igala people had trade with European but in 1841, Attah Ameh Ocheje signed the treaty on the abolition of the slave trade and the trade in palm produce was still at infantry stage and as such, could not sustain the Igala state economy which was initially dependent on the slave economy. This made it practically difficult for the Igala kingdom to sustain itself.

CHAPTER 6

BRITISH COLONIAL TRADE IN IGALA-LAND

The Igala economy underwent change once the transatlantic slave trade was abolished in 1807, which further changed the patterns of commerce between Igala and Europe. Thus, the formerly impure traffic in persons was replaced by the lawful trade in cash crops like palm oil and kernel, cotton, ivory, and other valuable minerals. As a result, European businesses, particularly those based in British industrial complexes in Liverpool, Manchester, Newcastle, and Bristol, among other locations, had a huge need for palm kernels. By the end of the seventh decade of the nineteenth century, Abdullahi Y. Musa claims the whole Niger-Benue confluence territories, including the Igala, had active economic exchanges with European nations. The need for a reliable supply source and a ready market resulted in the necessity to stifle trade rivalries and economic conflicts among the many trading enterprises. For instance, the first European steamships with the names "Quora" and "Alburkah" arrived at Idah by 1832. Captains Richard Landers and Macgregor Laird were in command of this trading trip.

When they arrived, they immediately saw the region's economic potential, particularly in palm products. Four British trading companies, the West African Company, the Company of African Merchants, Holland Jacques, and the Miller Brothers, merged to form the United African

Company (UAC) in 1879 and were placed under the leadership of Sir George Goldie Taubman in order to ensure that British economic interest was realized. These businesses mostly dealt in palm oil and palm kernels in Igala, among other things.

Soon after, the United African Company began to negotiate contracts with local monarchs to encourage positive trading relations with the people. By 1879, Sir Goldie had been to Idah to see the Atta Igala and the local situation. While attempts were made to promote and produce income crops, palm kernels were traded for European goods including mirrors, jack knives, cigarettes, and weapons. The business quickly established the purchasing station and secured the necessary certificates of occupancy. By 1900, the whole Igalaland and Nigerian settlements were effectively administered by the British, which also quickened the pace of the palm kernel trade.

Palm products started to get more attention from colonial authorities and locals after an efficient British colonial government emerged. They started focusing on the tremendous potential of palms, particularly in terms of improving peoples' economic fortunes. According to this viewpoint, efforts were undertaken to create palm plantations so that the benefits of economies of scale could be realized. Natives who had previously given their broad palm grooves less consideration started to change their minds. After processing, palm oil was traditionally the property of the male, the family's head of household, but the palm kernels belonged solely to the woman or wives. Rarely did the guys have any input on palm kernel matters. It was frowned upon to witness a guy preparing palm kernels in the Akpanya region. Therefore, palm kernels have a significant impact on the health of Igala women. They bought lotions, clothes, paid for medical expenses, thrift dues, and in certain instances, purchased food ingredients using the proceeds from the sale of palm kernels.

The consistent supply of nuts from Igala-land to Britain was based on a fair and efficient trading system. But reaching this objective depended on a number of interrelated circumstances. These included, among other things, a reliable transportation system, a safe environment where rules and order are upheld, and legislative and body aspects that were essential for the assembly and transit of the production to Europe.

For the transportation of people and nuts in particular, an efficient transit infrastructure was needed. Although rivers, pack animals, and head porters had been the main forms of transportation since before the arrival of the Europeans, they weren't utilised to their full potential, especially when it came to entering deep landlocked areas. This motivated colonial officials to start planning for the creation of road networks. The number of roads in Igala territory had hyperinflated by 1926. Community labor was used. The 29-mile Etobe-Ejule-Akpanya road was rebuilt in the same calendar year.

The Idah-Adoru-Nsukka road and the one-mile Idah-Onale roads were constructed by 1927. The eleven-mile Ankpa-Adoka road was expanded and upgraded, putting a motor in place. There were both forced labor and group labors. The arduous responsibility of maintaining constant peace and calm on these roadways and across the whole area was placed on each country and local government police. By 1926, the mercantilist businesses in Igala-land had embraced John Holt and the United African Company. These businesses controlled the trade of alternative cash crops and palm kernels. The indigenous were negatively impacted by this palm kernel trade monopoly because it prevented them from successfully lowering prices and bound them to the whims and caprices of the small number of customers. The mercantilist enterprises used local intermediaries to access distant areas of Igala-land. The local middlemen, known locally as Achanyama, were often a small group of people with sound financial positions who had forged connections with mercantilism firms to provide them with palm products.

At rates lower than those set by the purchasing stations, they acquire palm manufacturing. By 1955, intermediaries were paying 24 pounds per ton of nuts rather than the 28 pounds that were being paid at Onitsha. They assert that three pounds is the standard cost of shipping food from Ankpa to Onitsha. Considered in light of the significant exports, this profit is not insignificant. The intermediaries who traveled through and into the most distant areas of Igala-land were officially employed as contractors by mercantilist corporations. They go from home to house asking people about the availability of palm kernels. They pay trustworthy consumers in advance. Many of them ride bicycles and often provide local farmers with market information, especially when kernel prices have fallen drastically. It should be remembered that scale was first made available in Igala-land in 1929.

The middlemen utilized baskets and plates before the advent of the scale and weight method of measurement to determine the amount and cost of palm kernels and other grains. According to oral histories from all throughout Akpanya, they sometimes forcedly enlarged the plate sizes (this particular basket or plate abuse for action palm kernels is known as "Ochupu Uno/Elikwo"). This aggressive expansion's main goal was to demonstrate that significant amounts of kernels were bought at reduced prices. They also gave consumers who would ask for an early payment a discount, in particular. This explains the intense hostility that scale's arrival in Igala country was met with.

Trade during the colonial period was distorted and slanted against the locals in favor of the British. Price was set to disadvantage Igala locals and benefit British businesses. According to the district officer for Kabba division, "It has always been the same strategy across Nigeria when determining purchase rates of cotton to ensure their availability throughout the season." Other than pricing fixing, even when there was decline in importation and exportation of products, the British colonial administration collected duty

The figures for a period of five years are as follows:

	Quantity.	Value.	Duty collected
	Centals.	Pounds	Pounds
1928	142,250.	533,425.	88,899
1929	101,497	341,500.	63,432
1930	106,944	224,700	65,837
1931	37,623	78,260.	23,511
1932	28,232	58,744	17,645

Source: (NAK). Lokprof, 211, Kola Nut Importation. 1930. pp. 2

The effect of the alteration of the Igala traditional trade system by the British and its replacement with the British trade system on the Igala people, are multifaceted. They include economic, political and social effect. Economically, the Igala people were "double squeezed." They had their produce underpriced and were also forced to pay more for imported goods. The British trade systems and policies in Igala-land contributed greatly to the economic underdevelopment of the region. Through the excessive fixation and consistent re-adjustment and most unfortunately, the media was totally absent to make the exploitation known to the outsideworld

CHAPTER 7

THE IGALA TRADITIONAL RELIGIOUS BELIEF SYSTEM: BETWEEN MONOTHEISM AND POLYTHEISM

Igala cultural legacy has the same viewpoint as African intellectuals who say that in the pursuit of knowledge, the past and present are equally important. The claim made by Boston that "Their manner of indicating that a thing belongs to the largest order of human experience is to remark that it was known to the ancestors of long ago, ibogijo igbele," is thus not surprising. An elder would therefore always respond, "Nwu k'am'atawa k'wa kw'iko igbele igbele d," or "This is what our ancestors told us from ancient times," when questioned about the origin of the use of "j."

The Igala people also have a belief in a trinitarian hierarchy of supernatural or divine creatures (God-Ancestors-Diviners). These creatures trump the status and obligations of the average man. The Igala people only recognize one Ultimate Being, despite the appearance that they have many. There is just a hierarchy of suprasensible entities behind what seems to be numerous. This Ultimate Being is the Supreme Being, also referred to as "the Being beyond human description" or "jchamachala." "Man cannot comprehend the nature of God." The moniker "the Great God," pronounced "j" gbkwugbkwu, is prominent among those of God that reflect his nature. These names, jchamachala and jgbkwugbkwu, must be written in their smallest form, j, due to their length.

Despite the fact that the Igala people find it difficult to understand the true essence of God, even if they tried, it would be impossible, he cannot dispute the superiority of a supreme being who is the architect of the creative order. As a result, the Igala people refer to this Supreme Being as "jkiny'amnwu duu," or "God the creator of all." African philosophers considered creation to be one of God's special creations. "Across the continent of Africa, creation is the most frequently praised creation of God. It is said that God created everything to illustrate this idea. It would seem that the Igala people of Kogi state have a stolen idea of God given their strong ties to the Yoruba, the Igbo, the Gwari people, etc. Despite influences, they nevertheless have their own peculiarities. There is a widespread belief in the ultimate God known as "j," but it is hard to tell whether this belief is a result of interactions between different civilizations or tribes. The Ultimate Being is often referred to by a name in African culture, but the spirits and gods that act as bridges between humankind and the Ultimate Being vary from one culture to the next.

The Attributes/Works of God Generally, In African Traditional Religion, the names ascribed to God are based on the experience of a particular people. Some names are personal and mean only God, other names are descriptive, that is, portray attributes of God. The works and the attributes of God go hand in hand. God's attributes however are not determined by his works. For example, God is good independently of what he has done for us. But human language and also the Igala contextualization has made it possible that we may say for example, 'God is good', because of the good things of life we have received. Some do not acknowledge the fact of God's goodness, not because God has not bestowed his blessings, but because they have not recognized the goodness of God.

The Igala tradition holds that Ọjọ m'ẹnwu duu (God knows all things). He judges a secret intention, both good and evil, that is why he is called akajọ ẹnyọ (the good judge). He is also called the one who bestows good reward (arọmẹ ẹnyọ). Ọjọ ki n'ukpahiu duu (God that has all powers) is also his attribute; Ọjọ odobọgagwu' could also be used in expressing the omnipotence of God. Ọjọ achele ki ma k'ichan; the one that showers gifts without any iota of arrogance, is also attributed to God. All these attributes of God have made the religious Igala man to acknowledge God's kingship. In the attributes, we see that man names God and through these names he gives to God, he draws closer to God. With all these attributes, it is obvious that the Igala person is naturally God-conscious. As it were, all these attributes are anthropomorphic: "The image and work of the human rulers tend to be readily projected on to the image of God." God is regarded as the life-giving spirit of man, the controller of man's action and the creator of all things (Ọjọ ki ny'amẹnwu duu). Ọjọ created everything and lives in the sky. Ojale (sky) is the abode of Ọjọchamachala. The ilẹ (earth) belongs to men, while the ọj'ọna belongs to the ancestors.

However, the practical effects of these two worlds are felt here and now. That is why God, in Igala culture, has given power to each one according to his/her capacity and they are to use these powers to worship him and to enhance the welfare of one another. Through man's relationship with those in the afterlife man has link with God. The ancestors were once living beings with flesh and blood. They were 'heirs' of the living and so it is believed that they have a duty towards the living. The ancestors therefore act as guardian spirits. The Igala performs his duty to the Supreme God and such guardian spirits (ancestors), not out of fear but out of reverence and devotion. God is not seen as an object of argument. God is, (Ọjọ dọmọ), He exists and we owe him worship

MONOTHEISTIC OR POLYTHEISTIC?

These various complications in the concept of God among the Igala make it almost impossible to classify the Igala people under a particular concept that depicts a form of worship, either as pantheism, polytheism or monotheism. The two likely terms to make our selections therefore are polytheism and monotheism. But is it possible that the Igala notion of God falls under the polytheist category? Properly speaking, polytheism presupposes a pantheon in which Ọjọchamachala would be one. But Ọjọchamachala is the Supreme Being distinct from other beings. There are no two Ọjọchamachala. Ọjọ ch'okate- there is only one God. They believe that God is one and also believe in the existence of several spirits.

The concreteness of man's ultimate concern drives him toward polytheistic structures, the reaction of the absolute element against these drives him toward monotheistic structures…" Thus, worship of a multiplicity of divinities is rated very high in the traditional religions of Nigeria of which the Igala tradition stands out as one. One thing stands out among them all, that is, the element of worship.

In classical polytheism, the gods in the pantheon were all independent of one another. One of the gods might be regarded as the chief, but he was never regarded as the creator of the other gods.18 This understanding of the concept of polytheism justifies the claim of the Igala in monotheism, since what appears to be many is just a hierarchy of supernatural beings. That notwithstanding, its distinctiveness from the classical polytheistic concept lies in the fact that the one who is the Chief of all gods and goddesses is also the creator. Idowu gave an example of a clear case of polytheism, which he described as "proper polytheism". Using an evident example of the Olympian situation, we have a system where the gods appear not to have transcended the realm of the universe of social cliques and inter-tribal conflicts. All the gods were of the same rank and file.

They also shared in the passion of men and used their divinity to compete with, and beat men up.

In the Igala concept of God, subscribing to Quarcoopome's line of thought, Ojochamachala is not of the same rank and file with other divinities. He is the Supernatural Ultimate that is beyond the realm of the knowable. He is above the pantheon and therefore not part of it. The divinities were brought into being by him. They derive their power and authority from him. The divinities do not end in themselves, but they serve as means to an end. A situation therefore may exist where the divinities, although deriving their power and authority from God, can be treated for practical purposes as ends in themselves. Another reason also is that the divinities are accorded regular worship, whereas God is rarely worshipped directly.

At some points in the Igala tradition, there are manifestations of polytheistic elements, as is the case with ẹbọ emọ, that is, oath taking. The ancestors, as already noted, are revered as gods meant to protect the interest of the human race.

The Igala tend towards an emphasis on concreteness on the divine as available to man. Yet there is also recognition of an ultimate which transcends man expressed in the Great God, Ọgbẹkwugbẹkwu. When the focus is placed on this God, it is appropriate to speak in terms of monotheism. "However, this monotheistic concept of God tends to be unstable. On the one hand, insofar as God is ultimate, he is unavailable for practical needs and thus tends to be irrelevant to life."This distinction between the concrete and the ultimate in the Igala notion of God is still very complicated. Like some tribes and culture, the Igala people have not escaped the tension between the ultimate and the concrete. They differ from others and among themselves in their specific attempts to deal with the tension

The Igala traditional worldview, and by extension African faiths, blend the concepts of unity and plurality, transcendence and immanence, into a unified system; as a result, the ultimate God is often the singular, omniscient, almighty, transcendent creator, father, and judge. Africans understood that the God of Islam and Christianity was the same as their own ultimate gods from the moment that they first came into touch with them. Although it is apparent that the African concept of God has evolved through time, it is unknown if African faiths were more or less monotheistic than they are now.

Its description allowed us to infer that there once was a period when the ancestor-gods weren't. When they turn into "living-dead," that is when they start to become divine. This implies that everyone who lives virtuously on earth has the ability to become a deity. As a result, we are unable to use the terms "proper polytheism" or "proper monotheism" as such. Since both concreteness and ultimacy are included in the Igala's conception of God. As a result, both the monotheistic and polytheistic categories are present.

REFERENCES

- Kwekudee-tripdownmemorylane.blogspot.com
- International Journal of Trend in Research and Development, Volume 7(4), ISSN: 2394-9333
- www.ijtrd.com
- Abdullahi, J. (2006), The First Nigerian People, Anyigba, Winners Studios
- Idegu,E.U(2008) Ata Igala the Great. Kaduna, TW Press and Publishers Igala People Wikipedia.
- Igala World. Home of Hospitality and Peace. http//odogbas-com/history.html Isiaq,A.(2008) Nigerian Government and Politics. Spectrum Royal Gate Publishers.
- Ndoh, "Pre-colonial Political Institutions in Nigeria" in Ndoh,C.A. and Emezi,C.E.(1997)(ed) Nigerian Politics. Owerri, CRC Publishers.
- Onucheyo, "A Cultural Renaissance in the Confluence" in Onucheyo,E (2006) Culture for National Integration. Kaduna
- Source: (NAK). Lokprof, 211, Kola Nut Importation. 1930. pp. 2

- (NAK). NAK/Lokprof,19,IgalaDistrictReport. 1927. pp.3
- Abah, and Nwosumba, "The Dynamics of Palm Kernel Marketing in Igala Area,Nigeria 1920-1956…." pp. 192-205
- Abah, and Nwosumba, "The Dynamics of Palm Kernel Marketing in Igala Area,Nigeria 1920-1956……S" pp. 192-205

- Northrop, David,Trade without rulers:Precolonial economic developmentin southeastern Nigeria.Oxford university Press
- London 1978:47, see also Henderson, R.N., The King in Everyman; New Haven and London Yale University Press 1972:78.
- Abah, and Nwosumba, "The Dynamics of Palm Kernel Marketing in Igala Area,Nigeria 1920-1956……S" pp. 192-205

- (NAK). Lokprof, 211, Kola Nut Importation. 1930. pp.2

Negedu: The Igala Traditional Belief System

J. S. Boston, The Igala Kingdom, (Oxford: Oxford University Press, 1968), p.84

GROCERIES

Ané Igala: Igala land

Attama: spiritual priest

Benin: Tribe of South South Nigeria

Ejubejuailo: pectoral mask

Etsu: King in Nupe Tribe

Gago: clans head

Idah: headquarter of Igala-land

Igbo: Tribe of South Eastern Nigeria and Among the 1st the three dominating language in Nigeria

Juku: Tribe of North Central Nigeria

Koto korfe, Ajakuta, itobe, Ankpa: LGA in Kogi state

Lokoja: Kogi state capital

Ochiokolobia: Youth Leader

Ogbe: Acting judge

Ogbede: Attah's court

Oje: cassava flour

Ojo: God

Ọjọchamachala: Supreme Being(God)

Okwute: ritual staffs

Omadachi: village head

Onu: the principal person or chief

yegba Om' Idoko: Ayegba the son of Idoko

Yoruba: Tribe of the south western Nigeria and Among the 1st three dominant language in Nigeria